MY HEART'S

Cry

Prayers *and* Petitions

MY HEART'S

Prayers *and* Petitions

DANIELLE M. CLARKE

gatekeeper press™

Columbus, Ohio

My Heart's Cry: Prayers and Petitions

Published by Gatekeeper Press
2167 Stringtown Rd, Suite 109
Columbus, OH 43123-2989
www.GatekeeperPress.com

Library of Congress Control Number: 2021949647

ISBN (paperback): 9781662921612
eISBN: 9781662921629

Dedication

I dedicate this book to my favorite guy, Donny (Donald Clarke). I thank you for every lesson you taught me. Thank you for your patience and gentle love. A special thanks to my kids, Dillan and Wesley, for sharing me and supporting me. Love you. Cheri, you are the wind beneath these spiritual wings: GMUS, HMUS. Thanks to my parents for their guidance.

Table of Contents

A Letter to the Reader

In 2015, I endured the worst season of my marriage. Heartbroken and desperate, I stumbled into a movie theater in the middle of the day to see a newly released movie, *War Room*. I ran home, wrote out my prayer, and posted it to my wall. Days passed, and it seemed as if nothing had happened. One night, as I wept, God told me to pray. "That's what I've been doing for the past week! Aren't You listening?" I yelled back at Him.

He responded, "Just like that."

"Just like what?" I asked.

His response shocked me. "I want you to pray to me just like you yelled at me."

It took me a minute to understand what He was saying to me. He wanted me to be authentic. Looking back, I recognize my initial prayers were scripted. I researched the "right" passages to go along with my requests. I threw in a bunch of "if it be in Your will" and "if it pleases You, God" statements. While the prayers sounded great, they lacked passion and transparency. They lacked vulnerability. God wanted my heart's cry. He was not looking for a contrived petition filtered through my intellect and advanced education. He wanted me to cry and yell. God wanted me to release all the pain I was hiding in my heart. He wanted my heart's cry.

While my children slept, I walked into the bathroom in the basement of my house. I shut the door, sat on the floor, and cried. My cry turned into a screech and then a scream. If heard by a neighbor, the scream I had released would have certainly prompted a call to the police. It was the pain of decades of trauma endured and ignored. It represented every perceived failure and disappointment. Most importantly, it reflected years of unforgiveness held mainly against God. So much of what I learned in church caused me to doubt my ability to harbor unforgiveness against God. Who was I to hold something against Him? I learned the heart cares not about what it knows to be true but rather what it feels. And for years, I had felt wronged by God. I considered myself the victim of His elaborate and often diabolical plan for my life. While the Bible assured me He would never leave or forsake me, I often felt ignored by God. Like a child whose parent is engrossed in their phone, I thought I did not have God's attention. If I had His attention, why did He not intervene when my marriage fell apart or when I was abused as a child? He was present but absent, busy tending to someone else's needs. And so, I screamed.

My scream soon turned into yelling. I launched wild accusations at God, some I am embarrassed to repeat. I told Him how angry I was at Him and how alone I felt in life. I threw in His face the many things I had done in His name and for Him. I even cursed at Him. When I finished, I sat in disbelief. I could not believe I had said those things. Even more, I was shocked I hid those things in my heart, ever present, just below the surface. I had carried the weight of this pain for so long, it had become my baseline. I could not feel it. On that bathroom floor, I cast it all on Him. I sighed, and then I smiled. "Feel better?" He asked as if He had been waiting decades to ask. I nodded to indicate "yes."

The bathroom was where I gave birth to my authentic walk with God. It was as if the weight I carried was hidden beneath the veil of religion and proper spiritual etiquette. I tore the veil on that day, but am constantly aware of how easy it is to find myself hidden behind it. I continued to write my prayers. However, there was a difference after the bathroom experience. I did not overthink my requests. I wrote what I thought and felt. My writing was unfiltered and pure.

In writing, I discovered the power of an intimate relationship with God. I could not stop writing. I woke up in the middle of the night and wrote prayers. They served as a sort of love letter to God. The prayers also helped me to process my feelings, expectations and requests. More importantly, they served as a memorial in my walk with God. Each prayer tells the story of a place I have been and where God has met me. When I look back at the prayers, I can rejoice over all of the things God has brought me through, and all of the prayers He has answered. When I am low and unable to form words, the prayers speak for me.

A few years ago, I found out an acquaintance was having a challenging time after losing twins during pregnancy.

As I thought about what bouquet I could send her, God instructed me to send her the prayers I had written. I struggled with that request, as I saw them as my private correspondence between God and me. God assured me they had been a blessing to me and could serve as a source of comfort and inspiration for others. I gathered them together and mailed them to California. I had no idea that act of obedience would eventually lead me to share my prayers in a book, but here we are.

I will warn you—there may be prayers that do not make sense to you, and some that may not apply to your specific situation. However, I promise you will encounter someone somewhere along this journey of life who needs them. Feel free to pass them along. I did not start this journey to write a book. Instead, these are a collection of my prayers bound together in a book. They are not refined or eloquent. These prayers are simply my heart's cry.

I pray these prayers bless you and your family. Most importantly, I hope you are inspired to write out your own prayers and petitions.

How to Write Your Prayers

1. **Be transparent.** God knows everything you want to say, so don't hold back. By baring your whole heart to Him, you develop trust in your relationship. He's waiting for you to say the thing you are most afraid of sharing. Don't worry about how ugly it sounds or how embarrassing it is. God knows and loves you inclusive of it.

2. **Be bold.** God is a big God. He's a God of big things. As my father asserts, He loves to stack the deck against Himself. If we can do it in our own power, why bother God? Ask for the miracle. Ask for the thing that scares you. Ask for the thing that will bring God the most glory. We often sell ourselves short when it comes to prayer. We ask for needs when He has already promised to supply them. But what about our heart's desires? Go big or go home!

3. **Be direct.** We often think our prayers have to go on for days. Not so. Quick prayers are just as effective if prayed in earnest. You can write a five-page prayer or one that is one line. Both will be heard.

4. **Be you.** Resist the urge to sound like your pastor or your deacon. Your prayers should sound like a conversation you have with your best friend. God wants to hear from you... not you doing an impression of your pastor. Let your voice be heard.

"Words from the Lord"

I, the Lord, have spoken. This is the day I have made, rejoice and be glad in it. Many will say they are glad, but many refuse to walk in the freedom afforded to them. Gladness starts with a recognition of what I have done for them. It is essential you recognize the very air you breathe is a gift from Me. When you begin to understand the depths of My love for you, then and only then will you be glad.

Prayer to Break Generational Patterns

Dear Father,

I recognize a generational pattern emerging between _____ and me. I speak to the demon who stands as the doorkeeper, each subordinate demon protecting this stronghold, and those who attempt to influence each level of the soul, mind, body and heart. I cast you out in the name of Jesus. You no longer have a legal right to reside here. My relationship with _____ is restored in Jesus' name. I speak love and healing to our relationship. I speak trust and abundance into our relationship. I speak healthy communication into my relationship with _____. In Jesus' name, Amen.

Personal Prayer

_____

_____

_____

_____

_____

_____

_____

_____

_____

_____

_____

_____

_____

_____

_____

Prayer Against Satanic Attack on Family

Father God,

In the matchless and mighty name of Jesus, I come boldly into Your throne room of grace and mercy. I do not enter defeated but with authority, for You have given me power over the enemy. You have given me power to stomp on serpents, to silence contrary voices, and to cast out evil spirits. The power that raised Jesus from the dead, and enabled Him to have victory in this life, is the same power that lives and dwells, rules and abides in me. I speak directly to the enemy. Satan, take your hands off of my family. Every plan you made and every weapon you launched is canceled in Jesus' name. You are a liar and a loser. I release warring angels to stand at the doorpost of my dwelling. I send link angels to surround our property and to dwell in every room in our home. You are defeated, Satan. God, I ask for permission to stand in the gap for my children and husband. I speak to my mind and the minds of my family, and silence every wayward thought. Every confusing spirit that has entered into or that is influencing our minds is silenced in the name of Jesus. Every door of negative influence that was opened is now closed. Those doors shall never be opened again. Our minds are sharp and focused, and we are more than conquerors. We are determined and destined for greatness in the Kingdom of God.

Personal Prayer

Prayers for Children

All your children *shall be* taught by the LORD, And great *shall be* the peace of your children.
—Isaiah 54:13 (NKJV)

A man's heart plans his way, But the LORD directs his steps.
—Proverbs 16:9 (NKJV)

Dear Lord,

In Your word, You promise that you will teach my children, and that they will have great peace. By the oath You have made with me, I ask that You teach my children how to discern between Your direction and their own plans. Teach them how to choose Your plan over their desires. Give them the wisdom to seek Your plan before they take action. I desire that they know love, and seek to please You by being obedient in every area of their lives. I pray they are consumed with living a life of obedience and full submission to You at the age of ____ until the day they die. I pray that neither (the other parent) nor I could persuade them to be moved from this path. I pray that they are examples of obedience to Your will, to everyone they encounter. I pray You are well-pleased with them. In Jesus' name, Amen.

I have peace offerings with me; Today I have paid my vows.
—Proverbs 7:14 (NKJV)

Dear Lord,

According to Your covenant, You promise You will teach our children, and they will live in peace. Lord, You are bound by Your word. Teach my children how to reject the false peace the world offers. Help them to distinguish between what is false and what is true. Help them to choose Your way. Guard their hearts from deceit and foolishness. Teach them how to walk according to Your word. Change their hearts to desire what You desire. Release them from the power of self-fulfillment. Teach them how to desire to fulfill Your will for their lives. Don't let them fall victim to the lure of the world and the lustful desires it offers. Let them remain pure in heart and in thought. In Jesus' name, Amen.

> And he has given us this command: Those who love
> God must also love their fellow believers.
> —1 John 4:21 (NLT)

Dear Lord,

In Your word, You promise me You will teach my children, and that they will live in great peace. I pray You teach them how to love people. Teach them to see people the way You see them. Teach them to obey Your commands. Teach them how to share Your love with everyone they encounter. Let them see Your face when they see other people. Let them know You love them and help them to feel responsible for passing that love along. In Jesus' name, Amen.

In my heart I treasure Your promise, that I may not
sin against You.

—Psalms 119:11 (NABRE)

Lord,

You promise that You will teach my kids, and that they will
experience great peace. Father, teach them Your promises,
word, and secrets. Teach them how to hide them in their
hearts. Let them recall Your word so they might not sin
against You. I pray the Holy Spirit quickens their spirits
when tempted with evil. Remind them of Your promises
commands. Let them have a desire to study Your word.
Let them love Your word and Your correction. Let them
treasure it above all else. In Jesus' name, Amen.

Be cheerful no matter what; pray all the time; thank
God no matter what happens. This is the way God
wants you who belong to Christ Jesus to live.

—1 Thessalonians 5:16-18 (MSG)

Dear Lord,

Thank You for my beautiful children. They are so gifted
and talented. They are so loving and kind. Thank You for
their lives, health and strength. Lord, please teach them
how to be content in You. Teach them how to be cheerful no
matter the circumstance. Teach them to be grateful. Teach
them to keep the joy You gave them. Teach them to honor

you. You promised me You would teach them. Please honor Your word.

'For even if the mountains walk away and the hills fall to pieces, My love won't walk away from you, my covenant commitment of peace won't fall apart.' The GOD who has compassion on you says so.
—Isaiah 54:9-10 (MSG)

In Jesus' Name,

You made a covenant with me. I know You are truth and Your word never returns to You void. You stand guard over Your word to ensure that it accomplishes what it was meant to accomplish. Please teach my husband how to love me and honor me the way You do. Teach him how to stand, and not walk away from me in any sense of the word. Teach him to be compassionate. Teach him to cover me. I pray our marriage is strengthened and our children learn to honor their spouses by our example. Teach him to love You and his family. Teach him to guard his word in order that everything he says is true. In Jesus' name, Amen.

Dear Lord,

Your word tells us to train up a child in the way they should go, so when he or she is older they will not depart from it. Father, help me to not lead my children astray with the way I treat them or with my words. God, I am flawed and I am sinful. But, Your Spirit seeks to renew me. Renew my mind and my heart so that I do not recreate destructive patterns in the lives of my children. Help me to act lovingly, and help me to respond in a loving way to them. Help me to be kind and patient with them. Help me to allow them to make mistakes. Help me to laugh more with them.

Satan, I see you. Now, I revoke legal right to you and all of your power demons, doorkeeper demons, death demons, and other demons of the soul, mind and body that cause confusion and rejection. You are dismissed and have no legal authority to dwell here. I come against you with the blood of Jesus, and in the authority the Word of God gives me to cast you out. Go back to the pit of hell. We are set free by the sacrifice of Jesus Christ, son of the Most High God.

Father, for every seed the enemy planted through my willing and unknowing acts, I pray Your Spirit works diligently to reveal and heal that ground. God, redeem the time so I may pour love and concern into my children each and every day going forward. I pray each positive healing word has the weight of 100 years. Let every positive word spoken arrest 100 negative words spoken. Help me trust in You as I parent.

Every evil spirit that stands guard over generational strongholds, such as the Spirit of Jezebel, I revoke legal right and I cast you out of my mind, and destroy your influence over my body and soul. I declare I am free by the blood of Jesus. You must flee and return to the pit of hell. Satan, you are a liar and a thief. I caught you, and now you must repay seven times what you owe me. Pay time is now. I demand you cough up everything you stole. I command you to release identities stolen over the course of generations past. Satan, cough up joy, peace, prosperity, gentleness, patience, blessings, love, integrity, fidelity, purity, kindness and health you have stolen from my family.

Forgive me, Lord. Help me, Lord. I want to be free. Help me to walk in my freedom in Jesus' name. Amen.

Personal Prayer

Prayers for Daughters

In Jesus' name,

Teach _____ how to see You in all things. Help her to see the beauty of You in everything. Help her to have hope always and to never doubt. Teach her how to speak life and not death. Strengthen her when the enemy tries to speak words of defeat. Teach her how to love with words. In Jesus' name, Amen.

Dear Lord,

I thank You and praise You for _____'s life. She is a gift to our family, church and world. I pray she knows in the depths of her soul how beautifully and wonderfully made she is. Bless her with the ability to know Your love toward her in the deepest of ways. Teach us how to parent her, and help us to discern what is needed and when. I bind spirits of complaint, bitterness, anger, malice, perversion, rebelliousness, wickedness, lust, pride and low self-worth. I pray peace in her heart and mind. I pray for joy in the depth of her soul. Cause Your love to flow to and through her. Help her to know her gifts and to use them for Your glory. Teach her as Your covenant declares You will. I pray she only becomes what You have predestined and preordained her to be. Cause those things that are not of You to fall off. I pray she is not plagued by sexual perversions, or unholy and impure desires. Keep her pure and blameless. Protect her from the hand of the evil one. Teach her to be a living sacrifice, holy and acceptable unto You. I pray she hides Your word in her heart. Should she desire to marry, I pray her spouse is a man after Your own heart. In Jesus' name I pray, Amen.

Dear Lord,

Your word directs us to raise our children in the way they should go. We must come to You to learn how to raise them. Lord, teach me how to parent _____. Teach me to love and take care of her. Give me wisdom, Lord. I pray for her heart. I pray she guards her heart at all times. Help me to teach her to love You above all things and people. Give her Godly wisdom at a young age. Bless her with understanding. Help her to control her fears and anxieties. Help her to quickly cast them all on You. Please remove nervousness that causes disease in her body and any deficits in her processing or thinking. I pray she excels in everything she does. I pray she loves prayer and Your word. I pray she remains a virgin until You send her husband. I pray he is a man after Your own heart and that he remains a virgin until marriage. I pray he is fully committed to You and her. I pray their marriage is free from abuse, adultery, and selfishness. I pray her womb is open and she is able to bring forth life easily. I pray all of her children are born into the covenant of marriage. I pray all of her children are free from disease and deficits, as well as mental, emotional, spiritual and physical abnormalities. I pray she always honors You with her whole heart and body. In Jesus' name, Amen.

Personal Prayer

_____

_____

_____

_____

_____

_____

_____

_____

_____

_____

_____

_____

_____

_____

Prayers for Sons

Dear Lord,

You created _____ in Your image. You knew what he would experience here on earth before he was knitted in the womb. Your covenant assures me You will teach my children. Teach _____ Your will for his life. I pray You instruct him on how to honor his body and how to treat it as a living sacrifice, holy and acceptable to You. I pray You help him to control impure thoughts. Help him to think on things that are pure and holy. I desire that he not struggle with sexual impurity. Please shield and protect him. Let him reject impure thoughts. Protect him from sexual addictions. Break every demonic stronghold in this area. Tear down, uproot and unearth every demonic seed the enemy has planted. Cancel every demonic assignment on _____'s life. Greater is He that is in _____ than he that is in the world. Help him to see it. Help him to know it. Help him to activate every weapon in his spiritual arsenal. In Jesus' name.

> All your children will have GOD for their teacher—
> what a mentor for your children!
> —Isaiah 54:13 (MSG)

In Jesus' name,

Please teach _____ how to be a man after Your heart. Teach him how to pursue You and Your holiness. Teach him to be a man of integrity. Shield him from adultery and

19

unfaithfulness. Teach him the importance of honor without experiencing dishonor. Shield his mind and help him reject the trappings of the world. Close his eyes to the things that will lure him away from You. Shut his ears to gossip and backbiting. Build up his confidence in You. In Jesus' name, Amen.

Dear Lord,

Your word tells us to train up a child in the way he should go so that when he is older, he will not depart from it. I pray for _____. Instruct (other parent) and me on the way he should go. I pray for _____'s heart. I pray it is pure. Lord, rout out anything that is not of You that has found its way into his heart. I pray he knows who he is in You. Help him find his purpose and value in You. I pray he knows You love and care for him. I pray _____ knows You will always be enough for him. Cause him to be an honest man. Help him choose what is Godly in every situation. I pray he operates in Godly wisdom, and that he always seeks to please You first. I bind every demonic root that has grown in his life. I cast down every generational curse and repeated behavior. I destroy the spirit of deceit and witchcraft that has or seeks to attach itself to _____. I destroy every sexual perversion and addiction that has or seeks to attach itself to _____. I take captive every ungodly thought and desire the enemy implanted. I pray _____ remain set apart for You until he is married. I pray You remove every ungodly woman from his path. I pray every whorish spirit be cast down. I break the curse of rejection and rebelliousness. I plead the blood of

Jesus over _____. I pray You send him the right wife. I pray she is a woman after Your own heart. I pray she remains set apart for You until she gets married. I pray their marriage is free from adultery, selfishness and divorce. I pray every child they have is born of their marriage. I pray they conceive without complication. I pray they never experience a miscarriage or the death of a child. I pray their children are free from birth defects, illnesses and diseases. I pray their children love You.

Help _____ to see what is important and to chase after it. Give him the wisdom he needs to please You. Give him the strength to apply wisdom in every situation. Give me patience with him as he grows in You. In Jesus' name, Amen.

> Oh, the joys of those who do not follow the advice
> of the wicked, or stand around with sinners, or join
> in with mockers.
> —Psalms 1:1 (NLT)

Dear Lord,

Let _____ be filled with joy. Bless and protect him. Shield him from the advice of the wicked. Help him to discern what is good and what is evil. Give him a heart that chooses good. Pick his friends for him, oh God. Sever friendships and ungodly ties to people who mean him harm or whose ways do not line up with Yours. Let his ears be deafened to their words. Keep him from the company of sinners, those who plot evil in their heart. Cleanse his heart so he does not plot evil. Let his lips speak life and shun death. Let him build up and edify those around him. Let his heart be toward those who are considered to be the least of them. Help him to speak kindly to those around him. Teach him Your ways, God. In Jesus' name, Amen.

'No weapon formed against you shall prosper, And every tongue *which* rises against you in judgment You shall condemn. This *is* the heritage of the servants of the LORD, And their righteousness *is* from Me,' Says the LORD.
—Isaiah 54:17 (NKJV)

Dear Lord,

_____ is a servant of the Most High God. He is under the covenant You made with me. Therefore, his heritage is set. No weapon formed against _____ will prosper, and every tongue that rises against him in judgment, You will condemn. When evil is spoken against him, I pray the truth shall be revealed. I pray every demonic attack be cast down, and that the enemy does not get one victory out of this. I bind the hand of the enemy, every cohort and principality. Satan, you will not succeed. Lord, every false accusation launched against _____ will be exposed. You will make his name great, and teach and lead him with Your wisdom. I declare victory over his life. I declare good success. I declare abundance and peace. Help him to be all You created him to be. In Jesus' name, Amen.

But his delight *is* in the law of the LORD, And in
His law he meditates day and night.
                          —Psalms 1:2 (NKJV)

Dear Lord,

Help _____ to have the mind of Christ. Help him to
spiritually discern things. Help him to be spirit-led and
reject the things of the world. Cause him to be a lover of
Your word. Help him to desire Your word at all times. Guide
him with Your Spirit and teach him to do of Your will.

He shall be like a tree Planted by the rivers of water
that brings forth its fruit in its season.
                          —Psalms 1:3 (NKJV)

Dear Lord,

I pray not one thing done or said is able to knock _____
from Plan A for his life. I pray he brings forth his fruit in his
season. I pray nothing is delayed, and everything the enemy
sends his way will be used to strengthen his ministry. I pray
You open his eyes to Please protect him from himself. Help
him to yield. Do not allow anything to go undetected. I pray
You shine your light on him so that everything he does in
the dark, that may hinder his growth, be exposed. In Jesus'
name, Amen.

Personal Prayer

_____

_____

_____

_____

_____

_____

_____

_____

_____

_____

_____

_____

_____

_____

_____

_____

Prayers for Parents

God,

Thank You for making _____ my father and mother. You knew the DNA it would take to make me and You carefully selected them. Thank You for their gifts and talents. Thank You for allowing me to have them for the past _____ years. Thank You for giving me a father/mother that cares for and desires the very best for me. I thank You because they sacrificed their personal desires for me. I thank You because they love and care for their grandchildren. Thank You for their generous spirit. Help them to feel safe in Your arms. Help them to feel loved and cared for. Help them to rest in You. Amen.

Most Gracious God,

Today, I purpose in my heart that I am going to forgive my dad and mom. I release them from the debt I feel they owe me from childhood. I declare that I see them through fresh eyes. I will speak to them with reverence and respect for who they are and the knowledge they have. I will not treat them like they are an irritation. I will not disregard them. I will not challenge them in unhealthy ways. I will treat them lovingly. I will look at them with love. I will treat them as if they are valued and honored. Help me to see them as valuable. Help me to know how to honor them. Help me to think honorably about them. Help me to give them the benefit of the doubt. Help me to trust them. Help me,

Lord. I cannot do this on my own. I desperately need You. I desperately want to be and do better but often struggle with how to change. I believe I can do this because I know I can do all things through Christ that strengthens me. In Jesus' name, I declare that my heart is healed. In Jesus' name, Amen.

Day 1
Honour thy father and mother: that thy days may be long.
—Exodus 20:12 (KJV)

Dear Lord,

Your word tells us to honor our mothers and fathers that our days may be long upon the earth. While I desire long life, my first desire is to be pleasing to You. I confess I have unforgiveness in my heart toward my mother and father. Father, forgive me for harboring feelings of bitterness and anger toward them. I recognize this is a generational curse, and I will break this cycle through the power of the Holy Spirit. This type of breakthrough can only happen with Your help and through spiritual warfare. God, I pray right now, in the name of Jesus, that You move on my heart and show me how to forgive my mother/father, as You have forgiven me countless times. Help me to forgive them supernaturally. I pray as You are working on my heart that You move on my mother/father's heart to enable them to supernaturally forgive their mother and father. I am a curse breaker. I am a liberator. My obedience will change the trajectory of my family's history to come. Because of what You will do, mothers, daughters, fathers and sons that flow from my womb will be best of friends and honor God together. In Jesus' name!

Day 2
Trust in the Lord with all your heart; do not depend on your own understanding. Seek his will in all you do, and he will show you which path to take.
—Proverbs 3:5-6 (NLT)

Dear Lord,

I thank You for my father and mother. Thank You that you have blessed them with beautiful minds, full of intelligence and reason. Thank You for blessing them with knowledge about many things. Teach them how to use the natural gifts You have given them in the way You direct them. I pray they do not rely on their own way of thinking, but that they learn to trust in You in all areas of their life. I pray they forsake their own way. I pray they hear Your still, soft voice and follow. I pray their heart is clean and free from pride, vain ambition, selfishness, deceit, and bitterness. These sins direct us down a path away from Your will and purpose. Help them to see the error in their way of thinking. Help them to see that their way is harmful at times. Help them to forgive You so they can trust You with their whole heart. In Jesus' name, Amen.

Day 3

For he raised us from the dead along with Christ and seated us with him in the heavenly realms because we are united with Christ Jesus.

—Ephesians 2:6 (NLT)

Dear Lord,

I know You have raised us from dead things and our former way of life. I also know in order for us to live as resurrected children of God, we must be free in our minds. I pray every stronghold that has been set up in my father and mother's mind is cast down. I speak Your truth to every area of their minds. I come against every lie Satan has presented and that my father and mother has accepted. I pray You shine Your light on those dark spaces and that they walk in freedom in every area. I pray they take every contrary thought captive and causes them to be obedient to Your word. Open the eyes of their hearts, Lord, so they may see You. Just as Isaiah was undone when he laid eyes on You, help them to see themselves. In Jesus' name, Amen.

Day 4

And God will use this persecution to show his justice and to make you worthy of his Kingdom, for which you are suffering. In his justice he will pay back those who persecute you.

—2 Thessalonians 1:5-6 (NLT)

Dear Lord,

I pray You teach my father and mother how to forgive those who have wronged them. I pray You teach them how to forgive as You forgive. Teach them to release every debt owed to them since birth. I pray they release all bitterness and resentment held in their heart. Help them not to feel the need to seek vengeance or to hold others' actions against them. Your word tells us that You will use those wrongs to perfect us. You also tell us You will repay those who have persecuted us. Help them to see the emotional weight they have carried all these years. Help them to be free of the bondage they has placed held on to. Help them to see they can be different. Help them to see that You have forgiven many things on their behalf. Bring to their remembrance the mercy and kindness You have shown them, and Your requirement that they share the same mercy and kindness toward others. I bind every demon and every stronghold and cast them to a dry place where they have no more power over my father/mother. In Jesus' name, Amen.

Day 5

But it was to us that God revealed these things by his Spirit. For his Spirit searches out everything and shows us God's deep secrets. No one can know a person's thoughts except that person's own spirit, and no one can know God's thoughts except God's own Spirit. And we have received God's Spirit (not the world's spirit), so we can know the wonderful things God has freely given us.

—1 Corinthians 2:10-12 (NLT)

Dear Lord,

I pray my father and mother yield to Your Spirit. I pray that they know You in a deeper, more intimate way. I ask You to reveal Your deep mysteries to them. Soften and mold their hearts that they might long for this interaction and intimacy with You. Let them not forsake the wisdom, instructions and love Your Spirit provides. Let my father/mother not lean into their own understanding, but let them depend solely on You. Help them to know and recognize all of the wonderful gifts Your Spirit provides. In Jesus' name, Amen.

Day 6

In view of all this, make every effort to respond to God's promises. Supplement your faith with a generous provision of moral excellence, and moral excellence with knowledge, and knowledge with self-control, and self-control with patient endurance, and patient endurance with godliness, and godliness with brotherly affection, and brotherly affection with love for everyone.

—2 Peter 1:5-7 (NLT)

Dear Lord,

I pray my father and mother's faith is in You and not in their own abilities. I pray they seek moral excellence over financial gain. I pray their moral excellence guides the type of knowledge they seek to obtain, and that they exhibit self-control in how they exercise that knowledge. I pray they are patient and endure long with those who do not have the knowledge they have obtained. I pray godliness guides my father and mother in their interactions with their brothers and sisters in Christ. I pray that their love for your people leads to a love for all. I pray they deal with all people in love and patience. In Jesus' name, Amen.

Day 7

All Scripture is inspired by God and is useful to teach us what is true and to make us realize what is wrong in our lives. It corrects us when we are wrong and teaches us to do what is right. God uses it to prepare and equip his people to do every good work.
—2 Timothy 3:16-17 (NLT)

Dear Lord,

I pray my father and mother recognize their need to be taught and led by You. You gifted them with a great ability to learn and obtain knowledge. When a person is intelligent, it is sometimes difficult for them to receive knowledge from others, even You. I pray my father/mother loves Your word.

I pray they have a burning desire to study it with the sole purpose of seeking to know how to be like You. Lord, I pray whenever they see or hear the Word, they can see themselves. I pray they first apply the Word to their situation, and seek to correct their behavior through Your power. Remove the veil from their eyes so they receive the correction You desire to impart to them. Lord, I pray their lives are transformed and that they are fully prepared for every good work You have set before them. In Jesus' name, Amen.

Day 8

Oh, don't worry; we wouldn't dare say that we are as wonderful as these other men who tell you how important they are! But they are only comparing themselves with each other, using themselves as the standard of measurement. How ignorant!

—2 Corinthians 10:12 (NLT)

Dear Lord,

Help my father and mother to use You as the standard for their lives. Help them to hold Your word as the goal for all behavior and thinking. Let them avoid the trap of comparison. Help them refrain from looking to the left or right to measure themselves. Help them to know that as children of God, our aim is to be like You. I know our eyes naturally filter out everything that challenges us, dismissing it in a way that tears it down. But those who we believe we are better than, we cling to and compare in an effort to exalt ourselves. Help them to see the truth of that in their lives. Open their eyes to the harm that comparison brings. Help them to lift their eyes to You. In Jesus' name, Amen.

Day 9
Avoid worthless, foolish talk that only leads to more godless behavior.

—2 Timothy 2:16 (NLT)

Dear Lord,

Help my father and mother speak on good things. Help them avoid worthless, foolish talk that leads to godless behavior. Help them use wisdom when they speak to avoid entering into conversations that hurt or harm their witness. Let their words edify, and let them consider what they say before they say it. Help my father and mother consider the tone and motive for all that they say. Help them to season their words with grace. In Jesus' name, Amen.

Day 10
A new command I give you: Love one another. As I have loved you, so you must love one another.

—2 Timothy 2:16 (NLT)

Dear Lord,

Help my father/mother to feel responsibility for those You have placed in their lives. Remove any callousness in their heart that causes them to feel no responsibility for those with whom they have problems. Help them to see You have called them to assist and to love those whom You have placed in their paths. Let them not forsake their call or responsibilities. Change their hearts as it relates to others. In Jesus' name, Amen.

Day 11
The temptations in your life are no different from what others experience. And God is faithful. He will not allow the temptation to be more than you can stand. When you are tempted, he will show you a way out so that you can endure.
—1 Corinthians 10:13 (NLT)

Dear Lord,

Help my father/mother to see the help You offer them. When temptation presents itself, help them to recognize the way of escape You provide. Give them the wisdom and strength to choose Your way. Help them to walk according to the Spirit so they do not fulfill the lusts of the flesh. In Jesus' name, Amen.

Day 12
When God saw what they had done and how they had put a stop to their evil ways, he changed his mind and did not carry out the destruction he had threatened.
—Jonah 3:10 (NLT)

Dear Lord,

Help my father/mother to see that they can change the heart of God concerning every situation in their lives through obedience. I pray they understand their lives can be different if they choose to be different in their thinking. Help them to avoid resigning himself/herself to the way things are or used to be. Help them to see that better is always available. Help them to identify the areas that require attention. In Jesus' name, Amen.

Day 13
Yet we hear that some of you are living idle lives, refusing to work and meddling in other people's business. We command such people and urge them in the name of the Lord Jesus Christ to settle down and to earn their own living.
—2 Thessalonians 3:11-12 (NLT)

Dear Lord,

I pray my father and mother turn away from idleness. I pray they stop chasing worldly riches. I pray they turn away from seeking their own way. I pray they desire to work to provide for their family. I pray they feel a responsibility to contribute to their household and find your call on their lives. I pray they let go of deceitful plots, schemes and other unfruitful behaviors. In Jesus' name, Amen.

Day 14

May God give you more and more grace and peace as you grow in your knowledge of God and Jesus our Lord.

—2 Peter 1:2 (NLT)

Dear Lord,

I pray my father/mother desire to grow in the knowledge of You. I pray that in their eyes, earthly wisdom pales in comparison to Your knowledge and wisdom, Lord. I pray You extend to them more grace and peace as they grow and mature in You, Lord. Help them to desire You more and more each day. In Jesus' name, Amen.

Day 15

Let me put it another way. The law was our guardian until Christ came; it protected us until we could be made right with God through faith. And now that the way of faith has come, we no longer need the law as our guardian.

—Galatians 3:24-25 (NLT)

Dear Lord,

Free my father and mother from the bondage of the law. Help them to receive Your grace and mercy. Help them to receive Your loving kindness inclusive of what they have done wrong. Help them to see the lack in the law. I pray they are free from legalism. I pray they be made whole through their faith in Jesus. Help them to extend Your loving kindness, mercy and grace to those in their lives. Help them to be quick to forgive and restore those who wrong them. Help them love their enemies. Heal them so that they do not have to carry the burden of pain any longer. Teach them how to turn hurt over to You, and release the need to protect themselves. Help them to be vulnerable in ways You require of them. In Jesus' name, Amen.

Day 16

Because of God's grace to me, I have laid the foundation like an expert builder. Now others are building on it. But whoever is building on this foundation must be very careful. For no one can lay any foundation other than the one we already have—Jesus Christ.

—1 Corinthians 3:10-11 (NLT)

Dear Lord,

Help my father and mother build a foundation on You. Destroy, tear down and unearth every foundation that is steeped in their own way—bitterness, pride, self-righteousness, unforgiveness and the like. Help them yield to that process so their hope will be built on things eternal. In Jesus' name, Amen.

Day 17

And may the Lord make your love for one another
and for all people grow and overflow, just as our love
for you overflows.

—1 Thessalonians 3:12 (NLT)

Dear Lord,

Teach my father and mother how to love as You love. Help
them to see where flaws exist in their definition of love.
Help them see where they are falling short. Change their
heart so they desire to love people the way You love them.
Teach them how to love and respect each other. Teach them
how to love themselves. Teach them how to love You. In
Jesus' name, Amen.

Day 18

For 'the one who wants to enjoy life and see good
days [good—whether apparent or not] must keep
his tongue free from evil and his lips from speaking
guile (treachery, deceit).'

—1 Peter 3:10 (NLT)

Dear Lord,

Direct my father and mother as to what to say. Help them
not lean into their own understanding when speaking.
Instead, help them see what needs to be said, when it should
be spoken, and how it should be delivered. Help them to see
that truth is only spoken in love and with pure intentions.

Help them use wisdom when determining if a thing must be spoken. Let their words always be seasoned with grace. In Jesus' name, Amen.

Day 19
So just as sin ruled over all people and brought them to death, now God's wonderful grace rules instead, giving us right standing with God and resulting in eternal life through Jesus Christ our Lord.
—Romans 5:21 (NLT)

Dear Lord,

Help my father and mother understand Your grace and mercy. Help them to see it is through Your grace that they are made whole and receives right standing with You. Help them to see that right living does not buy right standing. It is only Your grace that affords it. Help my father/mother know You love them enough to cover them with grace. Help them to receive it so they may give it away as freely as You have given it. In Jesus' name, Amen.

Day 20
Don't let anyone capture you with empty philosophies and high-sounding nonsense that come from human thinking and from the spiritual powers of this world, rather than from Christ.
—Colossians 2:8 (NLT)

Dear Lord,

Help my father and mother so they can avoid the snares of worldly thinking that persuade them to chase after monetary gain. Help my father/mother so their focus is on You and the things You desire for them to pursue. Help them to break free of ungodly connections and philosophies. Let the mind of Christ rule in their lives. Let their thoughts be transformed. I beg and implore You as I stand as an intercessor crying out on their behalf. In Jesus' name, Amen.

Day 21
Good planning and hard work lead to prosperity, but hasty shortcuts lead to poverty.
—Proverbs 21:5 (NLT)

Dear Lord,

Help my father and mother to be motivated to work. Help them to avoid misguided shortcuts. Help them to plan, and to plan to work hard. Help them to see schemes for what they are. Help them invest in the gifts and talents You placed in them. Help them to not sell himself/herself short. In Jesus' name, Amen.

Day 22
Looking at the man, Jesus felt genuine love for him. 'There is still one thing you haven't done,' he told him. 'Go and sell all your possessions and give the

money to the poor, and you will have treasure in heaven. Then come, follow me.'

—Mark 10:21 (NLT)

Dear Lord,

I pray my father/mother releases the one thing that keeps them from surrendering their whole heart to You. Lead and guide them to a place of acceptance and surrender. Cause them to let go of all they places above You. In Jesus' name, Amen.

Day 23

This means that anyone who belongs to Christ has become a new person. The old life is gone; a new life has begun!

—2 Corinthians 5:17 (NLT)

Dear Lord,

Please help my father and mother to embrace the new life You freely gave to them. Help them to release from their hands, heart and mind the old life that was crucified with Christ. Open their eyes to see all the ways they continue to hold on to it. Help them to see the harm in it, and help them to release it daily. Help them stay firmly planted on the road You have laid before them. Let them not turn around and long for that which is dead. Erase the blueprint from their minds. In Jesus' name, Amen.

Day 24

We can rejoice, too, when we run into problems
and trials, for we know that they help us develop
endurance. And endurance develops strength of
character, and character strengthens our confident
hope of salvation.

—Romans 5:3-4 (NLT)

Dear Lord,

Help my father and mother to count it all joy when various
trials come their way. Help them to reflect on the trials
they have experienced to see what they learned or gained
from them. And where they have not learned or gained,
help them to see what they missed. I pray they begin to
ask the question "why" and closely examine themselves
when trials arise in their lives. Help them to yield to the
process so their endurance will be built and their character
strengthened. Help them to build their hope in You. Help
them to lean into and depend on You. Wreck everything in
their lives that is not firmly established in You. In Jesus'
name, Amen.

Day 25

You who are slaves must submit to your masters
with all respect. Do what they tell you—not only
if they are kind and reasonable, but even if they are
cruel.

—1 Peter 2:18 (NLT)

Dear Lord,

Create in my father and mother a submissive heart. Break down every rebellion and contrary thought that has found its way into their heart. Cause them to desire to follow the leaders You placed over them. Help them trust in You so they may yield to instruction and correction. Help them understand they do not have to agree in order to follow those who lead. Help them speak soft words, and help them know You will fight their battles. In Jesus' name, Amen.

Day 26

Like newborn babies, you must crave pure spiritual milk so that you will grow into a full experience of salvation. Cry out for this nourishment, now that you have had a taste of the Lord's kindness.

—1 Peter 2:2-3 (NLT)

Dear Lord,

Help my father and mother crave pure spiritual milk in order that they fully experience salvation. Help them long for it every day. Help them live abundantly as You desire for them. Let them release things that will detract from their experience. Help them remember the taste of the Lord's kindness. Help them recall their first love, You. In Jesus' name, Amen.

Day 27

In the same way, the tongue is a small thing that makes grand speeches. But a tiny spark can set a great forest on fire.

—James 3:5 (NLT)

Dear Lord,

Help my father and mother understand and consider the weight of their words. Help them see the impact that their words have on others. Help them use words sparingly. Help them carefully weigh what they say and how it is said. Help them consider how You view their speech. Help them listen more than they speak. In Jesus' name, Amen.

Day 28

What you ought to say is, 'If the Lord wants us to, we will live and do this or that.'

—James 4:15 (NLT)

Dear Lord,

Teach my father and mother to consider You in all their ways. Help them not to go astray or on their own way. Teach them how to seek Your will and Your guidance in all things. Help them know You are in control and You determine their days and their path. Help them align their will with Yours. When the two do not meet, help them surrender to You. In Jesus' name, Amen.

Day 29
Since God chose you to be the holy people He loves,
you must clothe yourselves with tenderhearted
mercy, kindness, humility, gentleness, and patience.
—Colossians 3:12 (NLT)

Dear Lord,

Help my father/mother and me become friends. Remove
bitterness and strife from me so we may enjoy a mutually
beneficial relationship. Help us to love and value one another.
Help us to be close and cherish each other's opinions. Help
us to be confidantes. Help us desire to spend time with one
another. Help them be the dad/mom I have always needed,
and help me to be the son/daughter they have always
wanted. In Jesus' name, Amen.

Day 30
In their greed they will make up clever lies to get
hold of your money. But God condemned them
long ago, and their destruction will not be delayed.
—2 Peter 2:3 (NLT)

Dear Lord,

I pray You shield my father/mother's finances. I pray You
block all liars and thieves who seek to steal from them. Help
them be free of the schemes that promise fast riches. Help
them desire to do things Your way. Help them have wisdom,
and to operate in it. Help them be free from debt. In Jesus'
name, Amen.

Personal Prayer

Prayer Against Demonic Assignments

Most Gracious God,

By the power and authority given to us by the shed blood of Christ when He conquered death, we cast down every messenger used by the enemy to accomplish his demonic and diabolical plan. We specifically cast down every bird of the air on demonic assignment to carry provisions and instructions to demonic representatives. We cancel each assignment. We combat every plot and plan, and thwart every attempt to communicate through these birds. We ask that the angels of the Lord defeat and destroy every horse and horseman sent into battle by the enemy. No weapon formed against us shall prosper, and every demonic force that rises against us shall be cast down. I strategically come against spirit horses and horsemen, cutting them off at the legs in the spirit realm and aborting every mission the enemy has sent them on, in the name of the Lord.

Personal Prayer

_____

_____

_____

_____

_____

_____

_____

_____

_____

_____

_____

_____

_____

_____

Prayers for Finances

Jehovah-Jireh,

Isaiah 54 assures us that we should have no fears as it relates to finances. You have us. You are, by Your word, obligated to supply our needs. I lift up my request for _____. I know You will provide. God, I ask that You move mightily on our behalf. Let it be to Your glory as always, Lord.

All-sufficient God,

I confess that my lack of discipline has me weighed down with debt. My poor choices and my living beyond my means have caused me to go into debt beyond what I am able to pay. I ask for Your forgiveness, Lord. Forgive me for my lack of discipline and for being a poor steward over what You gave me. I am ashamed because I am in debt. However, Your covenant to me tells me I will no longer live in shame. I will no longer feel disgraced. I declare and decree every assignment of debt attached to my family is severed. I pray that my mind and my habits are renewed as well. I pray You will eliminate all debt miraculously because of my obedience in this area. I pray You will use me mightily to plant seeds all around. In obedience to Your word, I sow a seed of $_____. I pray the seed I plant manifests itself 200-fold in my life in the next 10 days. I pray You cause men to bless me. Isaiah 54 tells me I am to enlarge my territory and spare no expense. Tell me how to expand, Lord. Give me wisdom as I move forward. Your covenant assured me I will burst at the seams. I pray this $____ seed causes me to burst at the seams as Your word promised. God, I ask You to make it manifest in my life over the next 10 days. I pray You rebuild me with precious jewels and make my foundations from lapis lazuli. Lord, make my towers of sparkling rubies, my gates of shining gems, and my walls of precious stones. Teach my children, and allow them to enjoy great peace. In Jesus' name, Amen.

Father God,

You are a living God. You are majestic and just in all Your ways. You are beautiful beyond description, too marvelous for words. You are too wonderful for comprehension, like nothing ever seen or heard. Who can match Your infinite wisdom? Who can fathom the depths of Your love? I stand in awe of You. You are the Lord who guards His word to ensure it comes to pass. In Isaiah 54, Your word declares You will rebuild us. It tells us to spread out our tents and spare no expense. Financial bondage does not line up with this covenant. We have the following debt: (list all debt). God, You are a miracle worker. I know You do not do anything halfway. So we petition You to finish what You have started and eliminate the debt miraculously. I do not want to owe anyone. I have been obedient in some things and ask Your forgiveness in the areas where I have not. I am stepping out on faith in obedience to You. God, show Yourself mighty so all who witness will see Your greatness and how You reward those who trust in You. Blow our minds, God. Do the impossible, God. Let word of Your greatness flow through the earth. Let those who see turn and give You glory and run to be obedient to You in the future. Help us to trust You. In Jesus' name, clear our debt and bless us above measure. We see ourselves debt free and give You thanks as our faith has made this thing so. We commit to do the following when we receive this blessing: _____ _____. In Jesus' name, Amen.

Personal Prayer

Prayer for Church

Dear Father,

While praise and worship is to acknowledge who You are, and to give thanks and glory to You for all You have done, it also helps us. It lets us hold You in the esteem and reverence due You. It helps us to see who You are, and to respond in a way that is acceptable to You. As we gather on Sunday mornings for service, I pray that we acknowledge who You are. Help us to prepare for this time all week long. Move on our hearts and our minds to dwell on Your goodness, character, love and kindness toward us. Help us to experience Your love in an overwhelming way each week, so as we join on _____ (day of the week), we can pour out our love for You in a united way. You have appointed (leaders' names). I pray You bless them with a life-changing love experience. I pray they live lives of worship each day. I pray You cause to fall away relationships, opportunities, connections, entanglements, obligations and desires that do not line up with Your will and purpose for their lives. Break down walls that prohibit them from living the life You called them to live. Cause them to be all You created them to be in You. I pray Your Spirit abides in the sanctuary of (name of church). I pray the angels encamp all around it. I pray they stand guard at the doors to keep out every spirit that seeks to obstruct the praise and worship from reaching Your throne. I pray our worship be acceptable unto You. In Jesus' name, Amen.

Personal Prayer

_____

_____

_____

_____

_____

_____

_____

_____

_____

_____

_____

_____

_____

_____

_____

Prayers for Self

Dear Lord,

You are my father (1 John 3:1). You are Creator and Sustainer of all things (Colossians 1:17). You are Love (1 John 4:8). You are full of mercy and kindness (Psalms 86:15). You are a just and forgiving God (1 John 1:9). You love me even when I do not love You. You sent Your son to die while I was Your enemy (Romans 5:10). You are all sufficient (Genesis 17:1). You are all knowing (Jude 1:25). You are ever present (Psalms 139:7-10). I am Your beloved daughter/son (Galatians 3:26). You knew me before I was knitted in my mother's womb (Jeremiah 1:5). I am the righteousness of Christ (2 Corinthians 5:21). I am fearfully and wonderfully made (Psalms 139:14). I have the same power and authority that given to Christ (Romans 8:11). At times, I struggle to walk in authority. Help my unbelief in the area of professing judgment over a thing. Help me to release every weight that holds me down. Help me to release every encumbrance. Help me to identify everything that stands in the way of me seeing, hearing, and listening to You. I cast down imaginations and excuses. I lay before You every concern and every care. Help me to identify unforgiveness I may have in my heart. Help me to release You, myself and others from perceived debts owed. Help me to share love, mercy and grace with others, and help me to create space for me to receive it.

Precious Father,

I love You and acknowledge You as the head of my life. You loved me when I was unlovable. You saved me when I was Your enemy. I love You with all of my heart. Help me to understand the depths of Your love for me. I pray I feel Your love and that I always remember how loved I am by You. Let me not find my worth in anyone else. Let me not be led by anything else. Let my heart's one desire be to know You and Your ways. Let Your love flow to me and through me. Help me to make Your desires my desires. Help me love the things You love and hate the things You hate. Help me see people as You see them. Help me love people the way You love them. Help me serve people the way You desire for me to serve them. Help me surrender every area of my life to You. Help me to release everything to You. Help my heart to heal in the places where it remains broken. Help me to identify the scars so that You may remove them. Restore me, Lord. Build me up. Strengthen me where I am weak. Cover me where I am naked. Protect me where I am vulnerable. Help me to be everything You want me and made me to be. In Jesus' name, Amen.

God of Heaven,

I love You. My heart yearns for deeper relationship with You. I know You are always with me. But, I recognize I am not always in tune with You. Help me to see my slow drift as it is happening. Far too often, I recognize it after it has already happened. I find myself in that space right now.

I have taken my eye off of You and I feel it. Help me to direct my gaze upon Your glory and everything You are. Help me to see all You desire to be for me. Help me to have my mind set on You such that I will not be drawn away by anything. I commit to recall Your faithfulness to me every morning, and to convince myself of Your faithfulness daily. You are my sufficiency and overflow. I am lacking nothing in You and have too much to speak of. Let me walk in the largeness of this relationship with You, taking care not to leave anything on the table of blessing and abundance You have set before me. In Jesus' name, Amen.

Dear Lord,

Help me to wait on You. It is my desire to be in Your will. Order my steps in Your word. Let Your word be a lamp unto my feet and a light unto my path. I turn control of my life over to You. May Your Holy Spirit lead, guide and direct my actions, thoughts and words. Let the words of my mouth and the meditation of my heart be acceptable in Your sight. Teach me Your ways, Lord. Help me glorify Your name in all I do. I surrender my will to You. I will not seek my own way but will wait patiently on You. I bind manipulation and self-serving attitudes in my life. Instead, help me to cultivate the fruit of the Spirit. Help me display the fruit in my life. Help me trust You as You lead me out upon the water. You are my refuge. You are my strength. You are my very present help in the time of trouble. You are the source of my joy and my peace. Let my mind be free from confusion. Help me to love You more. Reveal Your purpose to me. Reveal Your secrets to me as a friend and a member of Your inner circle. Help me to know Your ways, Lord. Help me to distinguish between my plans and Your will. Help me to stay in Your will. In Jesus' name, Amen.

Dear Almighty, All-sufficient, All-powerful God,

Thank you for giving Your children power and authority over the enemy. Thank You for making an open spectacle of Him when Christ died on the cross, and was resurrected with all power over death. In Jesus' name, I am empowered to trample over the enemy. Your word tells us no weapon formed against us will prosper, and all who rise up against us shall fall. Your word also declares the weapons of our warfare are mighty through You, God, to pull down strongholds. Therefore, in the mighty name of Jesus, and in the authority of His blood that was shed, I cast down every principality, power, all rulers of darkness of this world, and all spiritual wickedness in high places that have, is or will come against my household and my family. I pull down every stronghold that has invaded the mind of my family. I tear down every thought the enemy is trying to exalt against the knowledge of God, and I command that it be made obedient to the word and knowledge of God. Satan, you have no authority, and you and your cohorts are dismissed. I renounce you in the name of the Lord. You are dismissed from every area of my home and every area of my life. My family is free from your influence. We are free from your control. Lord, please dispatch Your mighty angels to stand at the doorposts of my home. Let Your angels surround and stand guard so the enemy will not be allowed in. Search our hearts and reveal anything that has already allowed the enemy a passage into our lives. Help us to be quick to repent and to turn away from these things. Purify our hearts and minds so we can serve You completely. In Jesus' name, Amen.

Father,

I know You love me and watch carefully over me to ensure the work You started in me is completed according to Your word. You desire me to be whole, lacking nothing, free from bondage, and emptied for Your use. You are actively working through me to renew my mind so I can fully access all You have placed in my destiny. Help me to see mindsets that hinder my access to Your ordained destiny. Open my spiritual eyes to see the ways in which my mind needs renewing. Specifically, I ask that You show me all of the ways my mind lives in the past, wrestles with regret, and fails to trust You. As You make me more aware, help me to tap into the supernatural power that lives in me, to capture every wayward thought and fantasy. Help me to identify them, arrest them, and audibly speak truth to them. In so doing, I will begin to live in the present, appreciate what You have blessed me with, and praise You for what is to come. Help me release anxiety concerning what I do not have in the present. I trust that what I have right now is exactly what I need, because You are Jehovah-Jireh. Because You are Abba, all I desire that will bless me is available to me when my mind lines up with destiny. I am assured of this and will walk in it every day. I exalt Your word and Your character above my will and my thoughts. Complete in me what You started. I yield. In Jesus' name, Amen.

Dear Father,

There is a proverb that says bitterness dries the bones. I understand that what I think is a surface condition, one that has the ability to seep deeply within and go undetected. I also think about my daily cup of coffee and how I add my creamer. Sometimes I think I have added enough until I taste it. While it looks perfect, the taste is still bitter. Lord, help me to pay attention when something is off. Even when I look like I am fine to others, help me to know all is not well. Do not let me ignore the signs, God. Help me recognize there may be something lurking beneath the surface of my thoughts and actions. Help me process and deal with anger so it does not fester. Most of all, show me if bitterness has found its way into my heart. Give me the strength to forgive. Give me the strength to let go of past things that weigh me down. Help me to acknowledge what exists so I may move past it. Help me, Lord. Restore, revive and renew me, God. Heal me. In Jesus' name, Amen.

Father,

I acknowledge You as the creator of the universe and the sustainer of my life. You created me to worship You. You loved me so much You sent Your son to die on the cross for me before I was formed in my mother's womb. You are my protector, my shield, and my comforter. You see me and You know me in ways that I do not know myself. For this,

I thank You. It is my desire to know You. I want to know Your thoughts and Your ways. I want to understand Your plan for me. I confess that I lean into my own understanding and allow my desires to dictate my life. Forgive me. Teach me how to live for You. Help me to hear Your voice and to trust You enough to follow. As I have confessed Jesus as my Lord and Savior, I accept the gift of the Holy Spirit and yield to the Spirit to guide me daily. Align the desires of my heart with Your will for my life. Help me to teach my children Your ways. Help me to be an example to them of how to live a life that pleases You. As my life lines up with Your will, I ask that You open the window of heaven and pour out Your blessings upon me and my children. I have confidence that whatever I ask in Your name, You will grant it to me according to Your will. Where I doubt, help my unbelief. Strengthen me and cover me. In Jesus' name, Amen.

Personal Prayer

_____

_____

_____

_____

_____

_____

_____

_____

_____

_____

_____

_____

_____

_____

_____

Prayer for Surrender

Dear Lord,

Thank You for Your love and kindness. Thank You for loving me inclusive of my wrongs. I confess I have not surrendered to You. I am controlling. I think my way is better, and I want things done that way. I despise those who do not love according to my standards. I gossip about them and belittle them in my mind. I have done this to my spouse, my children, my siblings, my friends, my church members, my parents, and almost everyone else in my life. I beat myself up when I am wrong or I make a mistake. I am exhausted. I'm sick and tired of thinking I can change or control everything. It leads to disappointment. I acknowledge I cannot change anything. I am nothing but a small part of the grand universe You have created. You are in control. I ask that You help me to release control over my life and stop fighting against what You desire for me. Help me not to manipulate. Help me not to direct. I admit I am full of pride. I need Your grace to cover that. I love You. I know You love me. Help me to feel it and to rest in that. In Jesus' name, Amen.

Personal Prayer

Prayer for Deliverance from Controlling Behavior

Father,

In the name of Jesus, I come acknowledging that I have fallen short in my relationship with _____. I confess I have exhibited undue influence in their life for a long time. I have taken joy in playing that role. I ask for Your forgiveness. Help me to learn and love this new role I have in _____'s life. Help me to mind my business and to be a support to them. Help me to pray for them and to support them without pressuring them. I pray You mend our relationship and shape it into what it should be. Allow me to step aside while You guide them and lead them. Allow me to move so they can develop their own circle of support. Forgive me and help them to forgive me. Heal their heart. In Jesus' name, Amen.

Personal Prayer

Prayer for the Morning

Dear Lord,

I thank You for the call on my life. I thank You for Your love and mercy. I commit my path to You, Lord. Help me to walk in the way You lead. Help me to hear Your voice and to wait patiently on You. Help me to cease striving and to allow You to work. Give me wisdom, Lord. I am available for Your use. In Jesus' name, Amen.

Personal Prayer

Prayer for Forgiveness

Dear Heavenly Father,

You are merciful and gracious in all Your ways. You loved us when we were Your enemies. You sacrificed Your son to reconcile us to You. You allowed His precious blood to be shed so we could be made right. Your word tells us that if we confess our sins, You are faithful and just to forgive us and to cleanse us of all unrighteousness. Father, Your word also tells us we must forgive if we are to receive Your forgiveness. Help me stretch my love to include the ability to forgive completely. There is no love without forgiveness. Help me forgive all who have wronged me. Help me release people from my expectations. Help me to forgive myself for sins I have committed. Help me to understand and remember I am not perfect. I am capable of sinning. I do not have to be perfect. You have not called me to perfection, but to holiness. As You teach me, help me take responsibility for my actions. But, help me to no longer walk in shame. Help me to fully receive the grace and mercy You extend to me. Help me not to live in condemnation. Help me walk in the freedom Your grace provides. I am loved. Inclusive of my wrongs, I am loved. I am forgiven. I am justified. I am righteous. I am a daughter of the Most High God. He is well pleased with me. In Jesus' name, Amen.

Personal Prayer

Prayers for Joy

Most Gracious and Wise God,

You are the source of my joy. You are my sustainer, my protector and my provider. I love You with all my heart, mind and strength. I look to You, for You are my sole source. Your strength is made perfect in my weakness. You are my help in time of trouble, and my refuge in the midst of a storm. Regardless of my circumstances, I know nothing can separate me from Your great love. This fact is the basis of my joy. Your sacrifice and my reconciliation are the reasons I have joy. This world cannot offer me anything that can sustain my joy. Your love, grace and mercy are the only true source of joy. You command me to rejoice always. Give me the strength and awareness to live by this commandment. When my eyes veer from Your goodness, direct me to turn them back to You. Let me not worry about things, family and circumstances. Help me to trust You. I bind fear, worry and anxiety. Instead, I choose joy. I choose You. In Jesus' name, Amen.

Father,

I exalt Your name high in all the earth. You alone are worthy of my praise. With the first fruit of my lips, I will glorify Your name. You are worthy of my worship; You alone! God, give me an unquenchable desire to worship You. Let my praise and worship be pleasing to You. I desire to worship You in spirit and in truth. Help me to walk in Your Spirit on a daily basis. Help me to live in the truth of Your word. Help me to worship You at all times. I desire to live my life as worship unto You. Praise is not what I do; it is who I am. Help me to know how I should worship You each day. Guide and direct my steps according to Your precepts. Show me how I can worship You in each decision I make today. Help me to know Your will today. Open my eyes to every opportunity You set before me to worship You. Open my ears to hear Your voice today. Help me to not hesitate in being obedient to Your directions. Give me the strength I need to accomplish all You have for me to do. Let every decision I make, every word I speak, and every step I take be in worship to You. In Jesus' name, Amen.

Dear Heavenly Father,

It is because of Your grace and mercy that I am able to give You praise today. There is nothing I have done or will do that makes me deserving of Your unmerited favor, but You give it to me anyway. I am grateful I no longer see myself as I was or through my actions. Instead, I can see myself through the eyes of grace. I am redeemed! I am set free. I am a child of God. Satan, I will no longer walk in the condemnation that you place in my path to trip me up. Because you are a liar, nothing but deceit flows from you. I no longer accept your lies as truth. I no longer believe what you say about me. I will rely on my Father's word to transform my mind. God, Your truth is my truth. I trust Your word. I trust You, God. I bind every area of unbelief that exists in my mind. I bind every stronghold established in my mind. I come against it with the truth of God's word. May God be exalted and the enemy be defeated in my heart and mind. May I lift Your word above all things. In Jesus' name, Amen.

Dear Lord,

Thank You for Your love that abounds. Thank You for Your love that covers a multitude of sins. Thank You for preparing a way of reconciliation for us. Thank You for showing Your love by sending Your son to die for the sins of all people. I pray Your people humble themselves and pray. I pray they seek Your face and turn from their evil ways. Your word tells us that when we do this, You will hear from Heaven and heal our land. I pray for repentant hearts today. I pray the scales are removed from their eyes today. I pray Your word pierces all fallow ground today. I pray Your angels are dispatched to prepare the atmosphere around Your people. I pray they hear the voice of the Holy Spirit today. I pray there is a great shift in the hearts and minds of Your people. I pray Your glory fills every place today. I pray the atmosphere is so thick with Your anointing that all come to repentance. In Jesus' name, Amen.

Dear God,

I thank You for the gift of life. Thank You for health, strength and a sound mind. Thank You for every blessing bestowed upon me. Thank You for everything from which You have protected me. Thank You for denying my requests for things that would have harmed me. Thank You for every circumstance You have allowed to grow me. Bless me with Godly wisdom so I might discern Your will for my life. I pray this wisdom helps me to make choices that bring me closer to You. Remove anything that hinders my relationship with You. Lord, I pray that when You bless me, I honor the Blesser and not the blessing. Help me to not be distracted with the creation, but instead honor the Creator. If I begin to take my eyes off of You, quicken my spirit so I may refocus. Help me enjoy my family and all the joys and comforts of this life. But, help me to keep these things from overshadowing my relationship with You. Help me to remember You are the source of my joy and, apart from You, there is nothing. In Jesus' name, Amen.

Abba Father,

I come before You today desiring to surrender all to You. I was created to be a living sacrifice, holy and acceptable unto You. I acknowledge this is my reasonable service because of Your great mercy. Help me to surrender fully to You. I acknowledge there are areas I am holding back from You. I ask for Your forgiveness for any area of disobedience. I know You have plans for me to prosper and not to harm me. Your plans are designed to give me a hope and a future. These plans do not always line up with my plans for my life. Where our plans do not align, help me trust in You with all of my heart, and to acknowledge You in all my ways. Help me to not lean into my own understanding, so You can direct my path. I surrender my day to You. Let me not waste time on things that do not glorify You. Help me to hear Your voice directing me to my Godly assignments today. When

I start to veer off course, bring back to my remembrance this prayer. May You be glorified through me today. In Jesus' name, Amen.

Most High God,

You are the creator of the universe. You reign over all things. You are wise and just. In Your infinite wisdom, You instructed me to walk in the Spirit. When I make the choice to walk in the Spirit, I deny the flesh that wars against the Spirit. Because I am a leaky vessel, I am not always aware of when I am walking according to the flesh. I thank You that Your word gives me evidence by which I may judge my progress each day. If I am walking in the Spirit, I will display the fruit of the Spirit. Open my eyes today to see when I am not walking in the Spirit. The first part of the fruit is love. Your word tells us You are love. Help me to know You in a new way today. Help me to fully understand what love is in order that I may display it. Help me to show love to everyone I encounter today. Give me the strength to display love when I am dealing with difficult circumstances. Help me to rule over my emotions today. Show me how You want me to display love so that I do not define it according to my own standards. Let others see You through the love I display to them. Help me to show love to those closest to me. Let the love I show start at home. Please let love abound in my heart. Fill my house with Your presence because love abides in Your presence. Let everyone who enters my home experience Your love upon entry. Let everyone who encounters me experience Your love. Let love rule in me. In Jesus' name, Amen.

Dear God,

Thank You for being my all. Psalm 16:11 tells me "in Your presence is the fullness of joy. At Your right hand are pleasures forever more." I thank You that I do not have to search here and there for joy and satisfaction. Every good thing can be found in You. Joy is a part of the fruit of the Spirit. Having joy is not a choice. It is a command. If I choose not to have joy, I am choosing not to walk in Your Spirit. Help me to have joy today. In every situation, help me to count it all joy. Even when things do not feel good, let me find joy in knowing You are perfecting me. Let my joy be infectious. Let those around me feel the joy when they are around me. Let them hear the joy when I speak. Let them see joy when they look at my face. Let Your joy so saturate me that I cannot help but express it. Let my joy not be in people or circumstances. Instead, let my joy rest in the assurance that You are mine and I am Yours. I am Your treasure, and in me You have placed Your Spirit to accomplish Your goodwill. I will rejoice always. In Jesus' name, Amen.

Personal Prayer

Prayer of Gratitude

Father,

It is a good thing to give thanks unto You. You direct us to give thanks with a grateful heart. I acknowledge that at times I give thanks with less than a grateful heart. There are times when my thanks simply fill a place in my organized prayer. At other times, I give thanks because that is what I have been taught to do. My words do not always flow from a place of true appreciation. They do not always flow from an understanding or contemplation of all You have done for me. Today, I ask that You show me how to have a grateful heart. Teach me how to appreciate who You are. Reset my priorities so that my focus can remain on the things above and not beneath. Help me to place value in the things that are important to You so that I might be grateful for them. For the things of God are eternal. They remain constant. I can always be grateful for them because they do not change. Help me to keep my eyes on the eternal. I am often distracted by the temporal, which leads to a temperamental heart. Change me, Lord! Create in me a grateful heart. Let my gratitude direct my attitude. In Jesus' name, Amen.

Personal Prayer

_____

_____

_____

_____

_____

_____

_____

_____

_____

_____

_____

_____

_____

_____

_____

_____

_____

Prayer for a Marriage

So they are no longer two, but one flesh. Therefore
what God has joined together, let no one separate.
—Matthew 19:6 (NIV)

Dear Lord,

You created marriage to last until death do us part. It was
the first institution You created. Your desire for families
to remain whole far exceeds anything I could imagine. So,
I bring my petition to You for the marriage of (couple's
names). I pray, Lord, that You renovate each of their hearts.
Clear out past hurts, harms, wrongs and offenses. Help
them to forgive each other and to forgive future hurts
quickly. Lord, I pray they come to know You and develop a
personal relationship with You. I pray they hear Your voice
and respond to Your commands. Teach them to pray in all
things, for one another and with one another. Help them to
raise their children to love and honor You. I bind the hand
of the enemy who would come to attack and destroy their
marriage. Shield and guide them as they rebuild. Remove
negative mindsets, unproductive thoughts, and biased
cultural beliefs that are deeply rooted in their psyche. Let
(husband) learn to honor and love his wife and let (wife)
respect and cherish her husband. I pray they realize they are
on the same team. In order for this to happen, they have to
be on Your team. Help them to dedicate their lives to You,
and to seek You first in all they do. In Jesus' name, Amen.

Personal Prayer

_____

_____

_____

_____

_____

_____

_____

_____

_____

_____

_____

_____

_____

_____

_____

_____

_____

Prayers for Family

Father God,

In the precious name of Jesus, I declare and decree Your goodness in all the earth. You are a sovereign God, creator and sustainer of all things. You are the Alpha and Omega. All things begin and end in You. All things exist in You. All that is, is because of You. And that which is not, is because of You. As You love me and have made a covenant of peace with me, I bring my cares and petitions to You.

1. I pray against the spirit of perversion. This spirit seeks to make us deviate from who we have been called to be in You. It seeks to keep us from Your ordained path for our lives. I stand in the gap and command it to flee. Free us from its bondage in the name of Jesus. I declare we are free to think, speak and act according to who You have called us to be and not who Satan, the deceiver, says we are. Satan is the father of all lies. He has lied to us to confuse us. Lord, help us to see ourselves as You see us, so we will not be deceived. I desire for it to be done as I speak it. Come quickly, Lord.

2. I pray for the men in my family. Lord, make them to be men after Your own heart. I desire that they fall in love with You. Help them to be bold, quick and proactive in their pursuit of You, and in the protection of their families. I want them to desire to go to battle with the enemy. I declare they will teach and lead their wives and children. I declare they are leaders at home, at church and

at their jobs. I declare they are transparent and authentic. I claim their healing from every disease. I declare they will walk in Your love. I declare they are mature in Christ, quick to forgive, and speak truth in every circumstance. I declare they are comfortable with being who You called them to be. Loose them from any ungodly spirit and heal every emotional wound. I desire for this to be done immediately as I speak it. Come quickly, Lord.

3. I pray the women in our family are ones who love and spread joy. I declare they are free from the spirit of bitterness and complaining. I declare they see the good in everything and that they have no harsh words to offer. I declare they will give thanks in all things. I declare they will not rebel, but know who they have been called to be. I declare they are confident in who they are in You, and that they are pure in heart and remain steadfast in Your love. I pray they never suffer from depression, low self-esteem, mental illness, molestation or abuse. I desire that this be done as I pray it. Come quickly, Lord.

4. Deliver us from the bondage of complaining and comparison. I pray each of us learns to submit to You. I pray we are quick to listen, slow to speak, and slow to be angry. I pray we mature in this area and remember You are in control of all things. I pray we yield to You and never fail to give You thanks. I bind every negative spirit that attempts to take up residence in our lives. Free us from the spirit of manipulation, lying and deceit. I desire that You do this as I am praying. Come quickly, Lord.

5. In Jesus' name, may these requests be heard on high and done according to Your word. Amen.

Dear Lord,

I thank You for _____ . I thank You that You knitted us together in love and community. Thank You for the gifts and talents You placed in each of us to be a blessing to each other and to Your kingdom. I thank You because You designed this family. You put thought and care into crafting it. Not one of us is here by chance or happenstance. Help us to see each other the way You see us. Help us to treat each other with the same love and kindness that You extend to us. Help us to value in each other the gifts You have placed in us. Help us to never abuse, misuse or take for granted the gifts You have placed in us. Help us to be open to receive correction from You and one another. Help us not to allow offense to build a wall between us. Help us to be transparent and authentic in our dealings with one another. Help us to approach each other with love. Help us to release bitterness and unforgiveness, and help us to be quick to apologize when we have wronged. Help us to see ourselves and to be quick to examine our motives and our actions. Help us to seek Your face so that we may grow and mature in You. We bind pride, vain ambition, selfishness, bitterness, offense and unforgiveness that seek to destroy what God has joined. We declare we are a family that loves God, one another, and ourselves too much to allow the enemy to come in and separate us. We will love, we will support, and we will defend one another. In Jesus' name, Amen.

Personal Prayer

Prayer for the Men in the Family

Father,

Your word tells us You have not given us the spirit of fear, but of love, power and a sound mind. I bind the spirit of fear that attempts to influence (names). I pray each of them operates in love, power and a sound mind. I pray they never waver between fear and faith. I pray they always trust You and have the courage to do what You have called each of them to do, no matter the circumstance. I pray whatever has kept them from succeeding or fully surrendering in the past is removed in the name of Jesus. I pray they do not allow doubt to rule their minds, but that they capture every thought the enemy sends. I pray they always remember that You carefully crafted a plan for their lives, and no one can cause it not to succeed. I pray they remember that even when they have not followed the plan, You have the ability to turn everything around for their good. They have nothing to fear for You are with them. If You be for them, why should they fear anyone or anything? May they be courageous and bold knowing You are all powerful, and that they are safe in the palm of Your hand. In Jesus' name.

Personal Prayer

Strategic Prayers for Passion

I long, yes, I faint with longing to enter the courts of the Lord. With my whole being, body and soul, I will shout joyfully to the living God. Even the sparrow finds a home, and the swallow builds her nest and raises her young at a place near Your altar, O Lord of Heaven's Armies, my King and my God!
—Psalms 84:2-3 (NLT)

Lord, help me to long for Your presence. Help me to wake to seek Your face. Help me to recall the benefits of daily time spent with You.

God himself is in Jerusalem's towers, revealing himself as its defender.
—Psalms 48:3 (NLT)

God, help me recall how great and mighty You are. You defend and cover me. You are always with me. You are my fortress and my shield. Let this knowledge fuel my passion to trust and serve You alone.

A single day in Your courts is better than a thousand anywhere else! I would rather be a gatekeeper in the house of my God than live the good life in the homes of the wicked.
—Psalms 84:10 (NLT)

By shifting my perspective and valuing what is truly good, I rekindle the flame of my passion for You. When my attention is on other things, it causes me discontentment. This leads to a lack of passion to pursue You and to celebrate the things You have already given me. Help me restore the joy of my salvation, God!

> Whatever is good and perfect is a gift coming down to us from God our Father, who created all the lights in the heavens. He never changes or casts a shifting shadow.
>
> —James 1:17 (NLT)

Deceit or a lack of integrity kills passion for God. It separates us from the will of God in that it is contrary to who He is. The most relevant question is "why do I lie or deceive?" It is a function of a desire to avoid consequences or to persuade people to believe I am something I am not. It stems from a puffed-up or extreme view of what I should be. It stems from feeling like I always have to be perfect, and not allowing myself the time and space to make mistakes and to learn from them. It comes from comparing myself to others and feeling less than them. But, it leads to me feeling as if I need to prove to them that I am superior. It stems from taking the easy way out. It is easier to pretend to be something than to actually be it. However, the weight of being something other than who I am becomes exhausting. Help me to address and dig up all the roots of these behaviors. Teach me how to be the same today as yesterday and tomorrow. Help me to be a woman/man of integrity and to confess and make right when I fall into people-pleasing behaviors. Help me to value Your thoughts of me higher than those of others. Help me not to be one who values perception more than reality.

Dear Heavenly Father,

You are a gracious and faithful God. Thank You for hearing my prayers. Thank You for responding in Your perfect timing. Thank You for equipping me with everything I need at the appointed time. Because You are faithful, I acknowledge my times of unfaithfulness. Forgive me for the times You directed me to be obedient and I failed. Help me to remain faithful to You. In obedience, I come lifting my husband, _____, before You. You placed him as the spiritual head of our household. You called him to be a faithful servant to You. I pray You cause him to be everything You have designed and empowered him to be. May his one pure and holy passion be to know and follow hard after You. I pray You soften his heart and that Your love penetrates every fiber of his being. Help him to know Your love and accept it. I pray he knows Your mercy and forgiveness, and receives it. I pray he humbles himself under Your mighty hand so that in due time, You exalt him. I pray he becomes a man after Your own heart. I pray he becomes a lover of Your word. Grant him Godly wisdom and understanding to enable him to rightly divide the word of truth. I pray he forsakes all the ways that displease You. Please take away the taste for things that displease You. I come against the spirit of rejection, deception and rebelliousness. I come against witchcraft and idolatry of every kind that has taken root in his life. I pray he forgives those who have wronged him, and that You heal every broken place within him. I pray that envy and strife have no place in his heart. I pray his mouth only speaks truth. I pray You wreck everything in his life that seeks to exalt itself against the knowledge of You. I pray he does Your will. Develop in him a heart that loves prayer and understands the importance of it. I pray he walks uprightly before You and his family. Use him mightily to set captives free. I pray he knows You are the way, the truth and the life. I pray to please release him from every addiction and every ungodly desire. Teach him how to love. Fill him with Your joy. Fill him with Your peace. Fill him with Your self-control. I come because I believe You are able and willing to do this, so You will get all the glory. I trust You and look forward to great and mighty results. In Jesus' name, Amen.

Personal Prayer

_____

_____

_____

_____

_____

_____

_____

_____

_____

_____

_____

_____

_____

_____

_____

_____

Prayer for Special Event

Dear Father,

Your word directs us to follow Your commands as a demonstration of our love for you. Your word also tells us that without faith, it is impossible to please You. It is my desire to be pleasing to You. Please forgive me when I do things that displease You, Lord. Please bless me when I do things that please You. In faith, as I believe I was instructed to do by You, I have organized _____. I know this will bless Your kingdom and Your people from all walks of life. I know You predestined and preordained this wonderful opportunity. I am excited about what You will do during this event. I cannot say I am not worried. But, You tell me to cast all my cares upon You. So, I am casting my cares about _____on You. I know You are a faithful God. I pray You strengthen my faith so that I am not discouraged. Please send the right people to assist and attend. I pray that You allow this event to be everything it should be. I pray You get all of the glory. In Jesus' name, Amen.

Personal Prayer

_____

_____

_____

_____

_____

_____

_____

_____

_____

_____

_____

_____

_____

_____

_____

_____

_____

Prayer Against a Spiritual Attack

Father,

You are a God who hears and responds. You are true to Your word. You never change. You honor that which You have spoken. You are just and gracious. You are full of mercy and loving kindness. I pray new mercies fall down on us this morning as Your word directs us. You are the God who battles. You are Jehovah-Gibbor. You are mighty in battle. Christ died to make us heirs. Now we are seated in Him. I speak from the place of authority in Christ. No weapon that is formed against me or my family will succeed. It may form, but it will not succeed. God, Your word tells me this attack did not come from You. Therefore, I petition You to send Your angels to war in the spiritual realm, and to destroy every weapon, wielder and designer of those weapons that are formed against us. I know all I need to do is stand still and You will fight my battle. I thank You for the restraint You've given me to allow You to fight this as You see fit. I pray right now that every wagging tongue be condemned right now in the name of Jesus, according to Your word in Isaiah 54. In Jesus' name, Amen.

Personal Prayer

Prayer Against Afflictions

Dear Lord,

I thank You for Your word and for the wisdom You share with Your children. Your desire is for us to be free from every bond. I pray You open my eyes to afflictions sent by the enemy. Help me to release the desire for attention and behaviors that will draw it. Help me to not desire sickness or injury. Help me not to think according to those thoughts. Help me to be free to think positively and to celebrate every moment. In Jesus' name, Amen.

Personal Prayer

_____

_____

_____

_____

_____

_____

_____

_____

_____

_____

_____

_____

_____

_____

_____

Prayer for Motivation

Dear Lord,

I know the enemy would love nothing more than to get us to waste our potential. Help me so that I do not allow him that foothold. Help me avoid walking that path. Help me to be obedient when Your Spirit directs me to a path. In Jesus' name, Amen.

Personal Prayer

Prayer to Develop Love

Dear Lord,

I struggle to love everyone. That's the truth. I am self-centered and full of pride. I cast down pride and self-exultation. I lift You higher than everything today. You are love and I desire to emulate You. Help me to be love to my children and to my husband. Help me to be love to my coworkers and my staff. Help me to be love to my extended family and church family. Help me to be love to my parents and my in-laws. Help me to be love to those I encounter on the street and while driving. Help me to be self-aware. In Jesus' name, Amen.

Personal Prayer

_____

_____

_____

_____

_____

_____

_____

_____

_____

_____

_____

_____

_____

_____

Prayer for Deliverance from Unhealthy Relationships

Father God,

Thank You for my life. Thank You for loving me inclusive of my lack. Thank You for making a plan to restore me to You centuries before I was born. Thank You for the gift of Your son, Jesus, who demonstrated His great love for us when He gave His life so I might live. Your love toward me is powerful, all-consuming, unbreakable, eternal, unconditional and accessible. Although You do not have a physical body, You are always with me. You made me special. You took time and care in crafting me. Every decision You made in designing me was intentional and perfect.

Although my confessions are true and Your word supports this, I do not always feel it. I confess my understanding and my view of love is significantly flawed. I have based my concepts of love on fantasy. I have created in my head a reality that is unattainable outside of You. I recognize this is a stronghold that the enemy uses to keep me feeling less than, and to keep me in bondage to unhealthy relationships. I revoke the enemy's legal right to my head space. I revoke every legal right I gave him. I renounce every soul tie that was established between me and (list them all). Sever every ungodly attachment in the spiritual realm. Have mercy on me, O Lord, and free me from every chain in my mind and heart. I ask that You do a supernatural work in me this moment. Heal my heart and help me to see with spiritual eyes. Help me to feel Your love and be made whole. Help me to see me as You see me. Help me not to settle for what the world offers. Help me to trust that You have plans for me and those plans will not harm me.

I ask that You send my angels, the ones that are assigned to war in the Spirit on my behalf, to go to war with every demonic force that has an assignment with my name on it. I cancel every assignment in the name of Jesus. I capture every wayward thought that enters my mind. Send Your angels to surround my home so that no one and nothing can penetrate the hedge of protection unless sent by You. Every demonic altar set up to thwart my complete deliverance is destroyed by the blood of Jesus. I have the victory in this battle because of the shed blood of Jesus. It is finished. It is done. In Jesus' name, Amen.

Personal Prayer

Closing Prayer for You

Most Gracious Father,

Thank You for Your faithfulness and Your loving kindness. Thank You for the person reading this prayer. Thank You for their life and their desire to draw near to You. May they experience You in a new way. Open their eyes to see You in every situation, and let them hear Your voice gently guiding them. Help them to know Your ways and to align their desires with Yours as they delight themselves in You. Teach them how to trust in You. Show them how to lean into You, and how to be transparent as they communicate with You. Assure them that nothing catches You by surprise, and that You love them. Walk with them as they develop a more intimate relationship with You, and reward them for their diligence as You have promised in Your word. Let no weapon formed against them prosper, and silence every tongue that rises up in judgment against them. Increase their capacity to love the things You love, and fill them with an unspeakable joy. In Jesus' name, Amen.

Personal Prayer

_____

_____

_____

_____

_____

_____

_____

_____

_____

_____

_____

_____

_____

_____

_____

Made in the USA
Middletown, DE
11 February 2022

60987412R00087